“

In the early days, when I created the little company that would become IDEO, we relied on trusted friends and family to try our prototypes and tell us what we needed to fix. It was an open, natural, and enjoyable way to make sure we were making stuff that worked for other people. Now we’ve grown, and so has the reach and scope of design. The range of people who inspire and inform us has expanded way beyond folks we already know. But we’ve kept that same spirit. We strive for that same trust-based way of collaborating with people.

— David Kelley

The Little Book of Design Research Ethics

By IDEO

1st Edition

ISBN 978-0-578-16303-1

The Little Book of

Design Research Ethics

Welcome

Welcome to another Little Book. This one is about ethical practices in design research. It covers the principles that guide our interactions as we search for insight. It's written for everyone at IDEO and for all the people we work with—those we learn from, and those we teach.

These principles aren't new to IDEO. Trust and collaboration are essential to our work; so respect, responsibility, and honesty have always been core to our culture. Empathy and cultural sensitivity are routine practice—we're human-centered designers after all!

What *is* new is the concise format you now hold in your hands. Constructing this book has been a major undertaking, with lots of soul-searching to strike a helpful balance between guidance, rules, and tools.

Across multiple locations, organizations, and disciplines, many more than 100 IDEO colleagues have given input to this book. We've distilled lessons learned—as you'll see, sometimes the hard way—from more than a quarter-century of experience and dozens of stories from the field. We've integrated advice and recommendations from external sources too—from ethicists and from existing codes of ethics in related professions, such as journalism and market research.

As IDEO's activities scale to create impact across the world, what's important to me is keeping a positive human experience at the heart of our purpose. Not only in the change we create, but also in the way we seek precious insight to inform that change. Beyond the basic tenet of doing no harm, we aspire to make people's experiences with us as enjoyable and mutually beneficial as possible.

Ideally this book will encourage us all to openly reflect on the issues that arise as we navigate the evolving and complex terrain of design research. And knowing that no set of guidelines can possibly anticipate all the challenging moments ahead, I'd like you to remember this:

If you're feeling uncertain, or nervous, or even just a little weird about something, know that you don't have to handle it on your own. Instead, reach out for support and advice from experienced colleagues, your design research leads, or IDEO's legal counsel, so that you can be confident your interpretation reflects the spirit at IDEO's core—the human-centered culture we've built together over many decades.

May your insights continue to enlighten us all!

Cheers,

Jane

Jane Fulton Suri

About This Book

"Well," you might ask, "if we're already embracing the principles, why do we need a book?"

Here's why:

To support great work

The quality of our work depends in large part upon people's willingness to share their time and energy as well as their deepest thoughts and feelings. This access is a privilege founded on trust—a fragile existence we betray at our peril. Being explicit about our ethical principles and guidelines helps to preserve this trust.

To make the abstract concrete

Respect, responsibility, and honesty sound great. But they're big abstract ideas that seem completely clear until we're asked to define and apply them in the complicated, messy, human situations of real life. This book aims to provide practical guidance we can use in the work we do every day.

To provide a shared reference

Common standards and language help us communicate our ethical priorities and think through the inevitable dilemmas that arise. An ongoing conversation that provides the opportunity to reflect together over time—not just during high-pressure moments when something doesn't feel right—allows us to leverage our shared knowledge and experience.

To build from in the future

Written principles and guidelines give us points of reference for the ethical challenges that accompany new opportunities for research. For example, the rise of social media offers a host of opportunities to track people's behavior; but those opportunities also raise new challenges around privacy. And new sources of information, such as sensors monitoring activity and habits, will challenge us to remember that real people stand behind what those devices reveal. Adapting to changes like these will be vital.

The book contains three principles and a set of guidelines.

The *principles*—respect, responsibility, and honesty—are persistent and fundamental.

The *guidelines* are the recommended actions embodying those principles. They guide us throughout a project—from planning our search for insight, to conducting activities in the field, to communicating what we've learned, to finally safekeeping the materials we've gathered.

To illustrate the principles in practice, there is a collection of real-world stories about challenges we've faced and the lessons we've learned.

An important note about what this book is not...

It does not provide legal advice. In general we'd expect to hold our ethical behavior to a higher standard than the law requires, but there are local laws that apply to our work. For example, there are laws regarding individuals' data protection, interactions with children, health and medical information, and, in some countries, information regarding an individual's sexual orientation or religious or political beliefs. Your local legal team and design researchers will be able to advise on this.

Neither does the book offer specific advice for best practices in different cultures and geographies around issues such as consent forms or compensation. If you're visiting an unfamiliar country or region, seek input from IDEO design researchers worldwide with experience working in those locations.

The Principles

Respect

Responsibility

Honesty

Consider:

Am I treating our participants as people—as collaborators—rather than subjects? Am I aware and considerate of the cultural expectations and sensitivities at play? Are my actions thoughtful and kind?

Respect

We honor participants' limits and value their comfort.

Consider:

Am I confident that our research isn't harmful to our participants? Are participants aware of the consequences of what they've shared with me? Do I have their informed consent? Am I safeguarding information that might compromise a participant in some way?

2

Responsibility

We act to protect people's current and future interests.

Consider:

Am I doing my best not to mislead participants or leave them with false impressions? When and how should we identify ourselves, what we're doing, and the intended outcome of their participation?

Honesty

We're truthful and timely in communication.

The Guidelines

Planning and Preparation
Gathering Information
Using and Sharing

N

The Guidelines

The following guidelines are the recommended actions that to the best of our collective knowledge embody respect, responsibility, and honesty in practice. They are organized roughly in the sequence of a project to make them accessible to everyone developing business, scoping projects, and doing the work.

Although they are tried, tested, and recommended, please understand, these guidelines should not be slavishly followed. They are not exhaustive, and will not address all the possible situations we'll face. Our work is dynamic and edgy—encompassing a broad range of industries, cultural contexts, and project types—and there'll always be a need for flexibility and judgment. Methods, tools, and cultural norms vary across time and geography, and our practices will evolve to fit.

As we work, let's use these guidelines to step outside our immediate concerns and reflect on a fundamental question: Is what we're doing respectful, responsible, and honest? And if it feels off, let's seek help and consensus to design an approach that feels right. An approach we can be proud of.

1

Planning and Preparation

We start our projects by designing research activities that will inform and inspire both our team and our client. At this early stage, applying the principles of respect, responsibility, and honesty creates conditions that provide a positive experience for everyone involved.

Keep the entire team accurately informed

Ensure that the team—made up of IDEO team members, contractors, and clients—is fully aware of how we conduct the research and protect the information gathered. The entire team needs to be clear about the rules around confidentiality and sharing information. In particular, our clients must understand exactly what can be shared with them, and what stays within IDEO.

Why It Matters:
IDEO's ability to gather the best information depends, in part, on our team acting in concert. We build trust by speaking clearly and consistently, and by working together to ensure the entire team respects and protects our participants at every point in the process. This also helps our clients communicate the process to their internal stakeholders and partners.

Seek support to clarify ethical ambiguity

Sometimes ethical questions occur about the best route to take on a project. Don't pretend to have all the answers. Instead, seek support from within the IDEO community, specifically our seasoned design researchers or IDEO's legal counsel.

Why It Matters:
Ethics questions are often complicated, so it's important to work together and align around best practices. IDEO has a strong and thriving community, with a broad range of research experience. Let's capitalize on our collective wisdom.

Give our participants clear explanation

Research should never feel covert or manipulative. We want to help participants make informed choices about what they share with us. We must tell them as early as possible—to the best of our knowledge—what the research is for, and how their information will be used, shared, and protected by IDEO.

The nature of our work means we can't always reveal certain basic elements of the study at the start of the research; but we reveal as much as possible by the end.

Why It Matters:
Maintaining a reputation for honesty is essential to our work and our clients. Transparent and respectful conduct helps build the best relationship with our participants, many of whom are our client's current and potential customers.

Seek permission, not forgiveness

In contrast to our internal convention, when we work with participants, we ask for consent, and encourage them to let us know their limits. Participants should always enter freely into our research, and should never feel pressured. Asking for consent as early as possible is important; and any interactions with a participant before they've formally opted-in to research should require minimal investment on their part.

Why It Matters:
Because we are often guests in our participants' world—a privilege easily revoked—we want them to feel empowered, appreciated, and respected at all times.

Our clients have chosen to work with us because they believe IDEO's human-centered philosophy can improve their organizations and help their customers. When we act with politeness and respect, we show that philosophy in action.

Keep your team lean in the field

It's important we carefully consider who is present during fieldwork. The study's demands; the topics being addressed; the space in which work is being performed; the cultural norms involved; participants' familiarity with our approach—all these should be taken into account.

Experience suggests two observers are generally best, and three a practical maximum. If more than two observers are needed, we ask participants if the larger number is acceptable. If there's pressure for more, it's worth considering alternative methods.

Why It Matters:
The comfort and ease felt by interview participants is a high priority during an in-context observation. For most participants,

it's easier to concentrate and relax with fewer people in a conversation.

Limiting the number of observers allows us a deeper connection with participants to gain higher-quality learning, leading to the most valuable insights for our project and client.

Questions to consider as we begin to plan and prepare:

» *Are we setting appropriate expectations?*

» *Are our planned activities considerate of people's time and needs?*

» *When is the best time to share who we are, what we're doing, and the intended outcome of people's participation?*

Respect in practice

Some forms of research—particularly those involving less face-to-face contact—carry a greater burden to anticipate a participant's vulnerabilities. These cases require additional thought and care regarding participants' emotional investment in the study.

Our client was a start-up developing a cancer treatment that would be an alternative to chemotherapy. To learn about how to communicate the treatment, we ran a large-scale survey with patients and caregivers to discover how they research, evaluate, and make decisions about cancer care. Everything was asked thoughtfully and gathered ethically. But people's write-in responses indicated that many wanted to know if this treatment was available and how they could enroll in a trial. Since this was a confidential survey, we had no way to follow-up with them. I felt bad that we couldn't close the loop. Next time, I'd avoid creating false hope among participants by communicating relevant information about the treatment and technology—in this case, the fact that treatment was still more than 10 years away.

COE LETA, DESIGN RESEARCHER

Responsibility in practice

Outfitting participants with sensors and recording devices allows us to track their activities and emotions as they go about their daily lives. We need to explain best practices to our participants as they capture data for us, and to carefully edit and protect sensitive information they may have recorded.

To learn more about how users consume non-professional media content at home and on the go, we asked participants to wear cameras and record video of their surroundings and activities. This helped us observe behavior directly and later review and discuss these visual diaries with participants. We gave verbal and written guidelines to our participants, explaining how to respect others while using these cameras. For example, we advised them to turn off the camera when interacting with anyone who had not agreed to be filmed, or to stop any time they felt uncomfortable capturing moments that felt too private. Of course, it wasn't always possible to do that—while people were shopping or driving, for instance—so we found we needed to carefully edit the diaries before sharing them.

SYLVIA, DESIGN RESEARCHER

Honesty in practice

Our preference is to provide full information before we engage with participants. But when such information would unduly influence their behavior, we get their permission to either not reveal particular information or to delay sharing it until after the session.

On the way to an interview, one of our clients suggested we introduce her as someone from IDEO. She was worried the participant wouldn't fully open up if he knew where she worked. She then suggested we say nothing and allow the participant to assume we were all from IDEO. As a regular client of ours, it was difficult explaining to her why I wasn't comfortable "disguising" her as an employee. The participant had already been told a client would be present. With hindsight I realized I could have done a better job of preparing the client for the interview by making it clear that we would introduce her truthfully, but without revealing her specific affiliation.

ANDY, DESIGN RESEARCHER

Honesty in practice

During live prototyping it's sometimes important for us to learn about people's natural reactions without their knowing at the time they're involved in a test. We share the intent of their involvement at the earliest appropriate moment, and answer direct questions truthfully.

We were developing future concepts for an online university program, and wanted to assess the level of interest in one of our new propositions. One experiment involved placing an ad for an unfinished concept on the university homepage and then counting the clicks to gauge interest. Anyone who did click got a pop-up window explaining the work was in progress, thanking them for their interest, and offering them a choice to continue exploring the prototype or leave the experiment. That way, we could gather information about initial interest and quickly clarify people's engagement so that those interested could willingly spend more time with us.

JOE, BUSINESS DESIGNER

2
Gathering Information

We learn from our participants by observing and actively engaging with them—in the real world and the virtual one. At this stage of the research process, the principles of respect, responsibility, and honesty are about considering the whole person, and the context in which they live—valuing their actions, beliefs, thoughts, and feelings as well as their limits.

Introduce the team accurately

When we make personal introductions, we don't lie or withhold information about the project team if the participant requests it. If we're concerned about introducing participant bias by sharing a client's identity upfront, it may be appropriate to ask the participant for permission to wait until the end of the session.

Why It Matters:
Our participants have a right to make informed decisions about those they allow to study them. This is especially relevant when we're entering their homes or workplace. By representing the team accurately, we offer transparency that helps participants feel comfortable and confident, which leads to more authentic interactions.

Listen, don't advise

Our research is about gaining people's perspectives, not about offering advice, opinions, or corrections. Participants should always feel their perspectives are valid, and not be swayed by any sense of deference that we are the experts.

If you see something troubling during your research, please seek advice from experienced design researchers or IDEO's legal team.

Why It Matters:
As design professionals, we are not experts in many other areas that may arise in the course of our research (e.g., medical

conditions, psychological challenges, or legal issues). If we offer advice that belongs in the domain of other experts and professionals, we may end up doing more harm than good.

Additionally, offering our own opinion or advice will influence participants during observations, muddying our results and making them less valuable to the project and client.

Don't make promises you can't keep

We avoid setting unrealistic expectations. For instance, prototypes, concepts, or conversations can mislead people into believing something not-yet-produced already exists. A clear explanation—either before or after engagement—can help avoid situations in which participants feel cheated by the outcome. Consider alternative approaches that could make their involvement more useful to them.

Why It Matters:
Disappointment could erode participants' trust, and create lasting negative perceptions of IDEO and our clients' new products or services. Participants may also crucially need the proposed solution being presented during the research. Deceiving them could delay their progress toward gaining alternative services or products that can help them now.

Take only the information we need

Today's technology—video, audio, photography, social media, and other digital resources—makes it possible to gather vast amounts of contextual information about a given participant, sometimes even without their knowledge. We must use restraint. We strive to stay focused, gathering and using no more information than is necessary to support the project at hand.

Why It Matters:
Out of respect for our participants, we avoid gathering information they haven't agreed to. This sets expectations about exactly what we will learn about a participant. Taking only what we need also ensures we can more readily identify valuable insights.

Questions to consider as we gather information:

» *Are we treating our participants like people, not subjects?*

» *Are there opportunities to engage in more open and reciprocal ways?*

» *Are we considerate of the personal and cultural sensitivities that might prevail?*

» *Are we making good use of everyone's time?*

Respect in practice

In enthusiastic pursuit of knowledge about sensitive personal topics—finances, intimate relationships, challenging health conditions—we need to be alert to subtle signs of discomfort that will cue us to change tack.

In field research for a project about dialysis and kidney disease, we interviewed a patient of important social and business status. Even though we clearly stated the purpose of the interview and gained his permission upfront to take photos, we somehow poked his emotional pain points again and again as the interview progressed. His discomfort built until about halfway through the interview he finally stood up and shouted he could no longer bear to continue. We were a little shocked but completely understood where he was coming from. So we wrapped up and left. I realized we should always pay close attention to the emotional reactions of respondents, and never force them into anything they feel uncomfortable with.

HELEN, DESIGN RESEARCHER

Respect in practice

When we measure the appeal of concepts and propositions, we bear in mind that real people are behind the data we're collecting; we acknowledge their participation in appropriate ways.

IDEO.org was working on projects to improve sanitation and build viable business opportunities in Zambia. One involved exploring the appeal of a latrine-emptying service to local villagers. To gauge whether people would realistically pay for it, we asked individuals whether they would sign up for the service—implying it already existed. Villagers were happy to do this, which was great news for the project. Unfortunately, they were infuriated later when we explained how the service was still only a concept, and they wouldn't be getting their latrines emptied anytime soon. Much later, we realized we could have delivered on the implied promise by arranging several days of service, rather than risk people feeling they'd been duped. Something we'd definitely do in future!

DANNY, SENIOR DESIGNER, IDEO.ORG

Respect in practice

Sensitivities vary widely between individuals, and we need to be careful not to assume our previous experiences or our own feelings will necessarily prepare us for the best ways to handle interactions. We adapt our approach to fit personal and cultural needs and customs.

For an IDEO.org project focused on early childhood development in East Africa, we began our research in Tanzania. We found the best way to understand the conventional wisdom in those communities was to ask mothers how a "typical" family in their neighborhood handled children's nutrition and health care. When we tried the same tactic in rural Ethiopia, it was far less effective, with each person responding, "I don't know." Because of Ethiopia's social norms around privacy, women were uncomfortable speculating about their neighbors' child-rearing practices. When we discovered this cultural nuance, we reworked our research approach to focus on advice the women had received themselves, avoiding any undue discomfort.

SHAUNA, DESIGN RESEARCHER, IDEO.ORG

Honesty in practice

How we demonstrate honesty can vary across cultures. It's important for us to understand those nuances.

Working with American colleagues, I've learned that honesty means stating everything upfront (e.g. that we'll be taking photos and video), and then asking people to sign an agreement in black and white before any research begins. By contrast, in Chinese culture, signing something in black and white is extremely intimidating, especially at the start of an interaction—it can make people feel they're being forced into a trap. To avoid this, we usually spend time simply talking about the details and explaining everything exactly as it's written on the consent form before the interview begins. Signing the form usually happens at the end of an interview. We've noticed people are more comfortable doing it this way as they've already built trust by experiencing the process. The principles are still followed, but executed in a more culturally accepted way.

HELEN, DESIGN RESEARCHER

3

Using and Sharing

As we make sense of the information we've gathered and share insights, the principles of respect, responsibility, and honesty dictate how selective we are about sharing and protecting personal details and information in our care.

Consider the audience

Think about who you are sharing information with, and why. Guard against potentially negative implications, even those you may not be specifically aware of. Consent forms often grant broad permission, so consider the context in which some forms of sharing could be harmful to participants or clients.

Why It Matters:
Long after a project has ended, the information we hold about participants may still have implications for their well-being. Participants often can't foresee all the possible outcomes of giving us their personal information, and granting us the freedom to use it for our work. Managing this information appropriately builds trust.

Represent honestly what we learn

Our deliverables frequently use people's stories and comments to explain our high-level insights and findings. It's important not to distort their words or intentions to fit a given framework or approach. We make inferences based on what we see, feel, hear, and discern, while staying true to an evidence-based point of view.

Why It Matters:
We are advocates for the authentic needs of the user; and representing our participants' needs truthfully helps us design

the most appropriate solutions. An honest assessment of those needs means our clients can better appraise the potential value of a given design solution.

Guard raw data

The goal of design research isn't to collect data; it's to synthesize information and provide insight and guidance that leads to action. We don't hand over unedited material—whether on paper, video, digital, or any other format. Instead, we edit and share insights relevant to the project, in the form of reports and other deliverables. Disclaimers on these deliverables should make clear the limits of repurposing or sharing this content.

Why It Matters:
Sharing irrelevant or unedited data can lead to unforeseen consequences outside the scope of a particular project, and carry potentially harmful implications for IDEO, our participants, and our clients.

Restricting access to data also ensures the client is well informed but without the additional responsibility of maintaining the agreements we have in place with our participants. This is especially important when, as often happens, clients later wish to share the content more widely.

Protect participants' recognizability and traceability

Unless we have direct written permission from a participant, we keep their personal information within IDEO only. We protect this information in all its forms; some less obvious than others. For example, we wouldn't share a participant's home address. Equally, we wouldn't share a blog they'd written or allow their license plate number to appear in a video.

Measures to help manage this may include using pseudonyms, asking people to disable location tracking capabilities on phones or other devices, or separating a participant's likeness from their comments to preserve their anonymity.

Why It Matters:
We want to retain the ability to attract people who are comfortable providing us with their personal information. We do this by maintaining our reputation for respecting and protecting participants.

Specifically, protecting medical and mental health information is a legal requirement, and must never be connected to the identity of the person. Even if we come across health-related information unintentionally, it's crucial we keep it separate from the participant's identity. We can share the story, but it should never be connected with the person's name (even first name), a photograph, or any other information that could identify the individual.

As an ethical matter, IDEO complies with HIPAA regulations, or local equivalent, even when working with clients or in territories where such regulations are not in effect.

Archive materials carefully

As we wrap up each project, we must delete sensitive information, eliminate or restrict cloud-based data, set access limits, and turn consent forms into our legal department for safekeeping. We make an effort to protect our participants always, not just for the duration of the project.

Why It Matters:
Archiving only what is necessary, and deleting all sensitive information that shouldn't be kept, reduces the risk of information being accessed or shared later in a way that could harm participants, IDEO teams, or clients.

Questions to consider as we work with information we've gathered:

» *Are we sharing what's important?*

» *Are we confident our documentation respects privacy boundaries and will not harm participants or their reputation?*

» *Have we adequately secured any physical or electronic records so that personally identifiable and confidential information is accessible to only those we intend?*

Guidelines at a Glance

Planning and Preparation

Keep the entire team accurately informed
Seek support to clarify ethical ambiguity
Give our participants clear explanation
Seek permission, not forgiveness
Keep your team lean in the field

Gathering Information

Introduce the team accurately
Listen, don't advise
Don't make promises you can't keep
Take only the information we need

Using and Sharing

Consider the audience
Represent honestly what we learn
Guard raw data
Protect participants' recognizability and traceability
Archive materials carefully

Responsibility in practice

Sometimes participants are so excited by their engagement with us, they offer unrestricted access to information they've shared. Despite this permission, we anticipate how their future opportunities might be compromised—even slightly—by the information we hold, and are selective about how and what we share.

We were designing mobile technology tools for young people diagnosed with schizophrenia. We interviewed a patient who was so inspired by participating with us he created a lovely song to post online. He was excited by the idea of creating links from his own website to reports about the study, even granting our client written permission to do this. It was tough to refuse—we wanted to encourage his creativity and not perpetuate the stigma attached to mental illness. At the same time, we couldn't be instrumental in allowing his identity to be connected to information about his condition. We discouraged him from linking to our content on his website, and promised to share the story about him as a talented and creative individual, but omitting information that could let others track his identity.

SYLVIA, DESIGN RESEARCHER

Responsibility in practice

We routinely remove names and other formal identifiers from data, but we need to remain vigilant when sharing it beyond our team. Information that appears to be anonymous may not be, especially when it comes from a population known closely by our audience.

As part of a cultural transformation project for a large tech firm, we conducted an initial benchmarking survey across its business units. We were exploring attitudes towards creative thinking, knowledge-sharing, and empowerment within the organization; and gathering biographical details such as business function, tenure, and department. While responses were anonymous, biographical details combined with language preferences for taking the survey would have "outed" respondents in smaller departments. Because of our commitment to protect respondents' anonymity, we did not share the full data set with the client, sharing only aggregate data and selected representative comments.

ALISA, RESEARCH RECRUITER

Responsibility in practice

Sometimes participants say or do things that communicate powerfully the value of our approach—iconic moments we wish to publish more widely. Careful recordkeeping ensures we can maintain participants' rights regarding public stories we want to tell years into the future.

Back in our early days, our team was exploring how new digital technologies could better support small businesses. We arranged to observe our travel agent at work in her office. She had no patience with the user-manual for her phone system and showed us her unique method of handling conference calls. We photographed her physically assembling phones on her desk, calling each person separately, and then arranging the handsets to facilitate a group conversation. This workaround helped her keep track of how callers were connected—clearly a design opportunity. Long after our project was over, she gave us her blessing to share this story in print. It became one of our most cherished research vignettes. We still show the photos and talk about it today—without divulging her real name.

PETE, INTERACTION DESIGNER

Honesty in practice

Being straightforward about communication extends beyond gathering information to include how we represent our methods and approach.

Our project was about the experience of purchasing newly built homes. We conducted three interviews in-context, each with a very different kind of buyer; and visited several show-houses ourselves to experience the process. Our client was happy with the insights, but with a big presentation looming, she feared her colleagues might not take the work seriously because of the size of the research sample. Could we somehow bolster our findings? We obviously weren't comfortable with the idea of exaggerating the scale of our research, but we didn't have the time or budget to gather more data. We recommended presenting the study as it was and, if there were doubts about the validity of our insights, we could later adjust the budget to cover additional research. During the presentation, we were quizzed about our approach. When we said we had interviewed three people, the CEO congratulated us, saying, "Well, evidently, you picked the right three."

DAVID, DESIGN STRATEGIST

Closing Thoughts

Explore and Evolve

The Little Book of IDEO talks about balancing grown-upness with childlike wonder—the value of placing "some boundary conditions and expectations on one another so that we can still keep the excited part of ourselves but contain the craziness."

Here we have those conditions: Ethical practices for design research. A touchstone for our conduct that has real-world implications for the quality of our insights, our design output, and the access to private lives afforded to us—now and in the future.

We've worked to make it feel just right, not too tight or too loose, too assertive or too apologetic. Through numerous internal discussions, we've balanced curiosity and the relentless search for good data and insight, with the interests of clients, participants, and collaborators.

Respect, responsibility, and honesty are timeless principles—criteria against which we will always measure our actions. Precisely how we uphold these principles in practice is likely to evolve over time in response to new conditions, new contexts, and new challenges. But this is IDEO, so we'll continue to break new ground and learn from the challenges we meet.

Keep exploring, stay connected, and we'll evolve as we must.

Reflections

Further thoughts on design research ethics and IDEO

“ *This is a good moment to be reminded what a human-centered design culture is about. I see a future in which design research will increasingly rely on data for insight, whether generated real-time through sensors attached to people, or from existing digital data streams. It's harder to take people into account when we never actually meet them. This book creates a foundation to support human-centeredness in that future.*

— **Tim Brown** *CEO, IDEO*

“ 'It took me four years to paint like Raphael, but a lifetime to paint like a child.' — Pablo Picasso

As new contexts, situations, and problems appear every day at IDEO, our ability to understand the formal lines we want to color inside and outside of is critical. Learning these rules and understanding them deeply gives us permission to play, abstract, and modify them accordingly and, of course, respectfully.

— **Paul Bennett** *Chief Creative Officer, IDEO*

“Every day, design research at IDEO continues to help more people get inspired by learning about other’s experiences and cultures. As we open up opportunities, we need to be mindful of unintended consequences, from making others uncomfortable to putting people at serious risk. Based on decades of collective experience, these guidelines and principles form a foundation for our practice at IDEO and far beyond.

— **Suzanne Gibbs Howard** *Dean of IDEO U*

“I strive to balance the needs and desires of my team and clients with those of people we study. IDEO’s explicit attention to ethics allows me to find the best research participants, and have confidence that all will be treated with dignity and respect.

— **Dorinda von Stroheim** *Global Design Research Recruiting, IDEO*

“In the increasingly complex legal and regulatory worlds of privacy and data protection, this Little Book of Design Research Ethics *gives researchers real stories, high aspirations, and clear guidelines for dealing with situations that regulations rarely, if ever, explain.*

— **Rochael Soper Adranly** *General Counsel, IDEO*

“ *The ethics we bring to design research are about more than standard practice. They are how we communicate our values out in the world, from New York to Nairobi.*

— **Patrice Martin** *Co-Lead & Creative Director, IDEO.org*

“ *At first glance, it appears that ethics and creativity have nothing in common; one is constrained and the other unbridled. And yet, ethics is the insider handshake to a world of unexpected delights and creative starting points. The secret to getting others to share their secrets is to conduct yourself with the utmost respect.*

— **Coe Leta Stafford** *Design Director, IDEO Palo Alto*

“ *In a region as big as Asia, you run the gamut of cities/countries that are ultra sensitive and respectful around privacy, and those who don't understand why there would even be a concern in the first place. As a firm deeply rooted in uncovering stories of inspiration from around the world, I could not think of anything more important than having a shared credo that helps all of us (our colleagues, clients, and participants) feel and exhibit respect, responsibility, and honesty.*

— **Mike Peng** *Managing Director, IDEO Tokyo*

“At its best, ethics is about what's possible. It's about creativity, justice, transparency, respect, honesty, trust. The Little Book reinforces these virtues, reminding each of us about what is important in work and in relationships with colleagues and clients. It's a valuable resource; encouraging us to be the best we can, learning about other's experiences—all towards a mutual goal of ethical sensitivity and reflection. Action expresses priority: IDEO shows clearly and pragmatically that ethics is a fundamental priority.

— **Elizabeth Buchanan** *Endowed Chair & Director, Center for Applied Ethics, University of Wisconsin-Stout*

“This is the most accessible document of its kind that I have seen. It is built on absolutely solid ethical foundations, and at the same time is immediately practical in the best senses of the word: it can be quickly referred to for examples of guiding principles that are both easy to understand and apply in practice. In these ways, the document should serve IDEO—both clients and employees—very well indeed. Moreover it is a model, certainly for design, research, academic, and other communities concerned with practical ethics.

— **Charles Ess** *Author of “Digital Media Ethics” and Professor in Media Studies, University of Oslo*